The Landscape of Britain

ROBERT HALLMANN
The Landscape of Britain

TEXT BY STEPHEN DANIELS

B T Batsford Ltd · *London*

First published 1984
© Robert Hallmann 1984
Text © B.T. Batsford Ltd, 1984

ISBN 0 7134 3735 9

Printed in Spain
for the publishers,
B.T. Batsford Ltd,
4 Fitzhardinge Street, London W1H 0AH

Frontispiece: *Loch Tulla, Argyll, Strathclyde.*

Contents

LIST OF PHOTOGRAPHS

Introduction

Britain has a kaleidoscopic variety of scenery. Its diverse pattern of rock and relief has been reworked by a long and complex history of human occupancy. Man has everywhere modified the landscape of Britain and in some places transformed it. Men and women have not done this in isolation but as members of societies with distinctive economies, technologies, legal systems, beliefs and tastes. Successive societies have imprinted their features on the land.

The effects of human action are most conspicuous in urban and industrial landscapes and most appealing in scenes of lush fields and snug villages where nature seems so agreeably fashioned for living in and looking at. In wilder places the effects of human action may be more significant than they seem. The solitude of Scottish glens is a human creation, resulting from a crucial change in Highland society. By the late eighteenth century the feudal relations between Highland chiefs and their clansmen had been dissolved by English military power and the growth of a market economy. Families were evicted from Highland glens to make way for profitable sheep. Careless grazing stripped pastures and cheaper imports of wool and mutton made the remaining sheep-runs unprofitable. Vast areas were reduced to that state of wilderness which is now so much admired.

In many parts of Britain no single society has imposed its design on the land. Occupants in different phases of an area's history have left their imprint. The appeal of these landscapes is their physical variety and historical depth, shown dramatically in the photographs which are the basis of this book. Consider the view of Widecombe in the Moor in Devon. Its interest as a historical document adds to its picturesque appeal. The boulder in the foreground is weathered out from the granite mass of Dartmoor. When exposed to the atmosphere granite breaks down to a thin

7

acid soil which can scarcely support trees or crops. But the rough moorland pasture we see is not natural vegetation; it has been modified by a long history of pastoral farming. This area of moorland is covered with standing stones and burial mounds, relics of prehistoric settlers who chose this high plateau in preference to the then forest-choked valleys. The valley in the middle distance was first cleared and cultivated in the Middle Ages but the patchwork of fields we see now is a creation that is less than two centuries old. In the mid-nineteenth century Widecombe was the centre of a livestock economy with sheep and ponies grazed on the moors and cattle in the fields. They were sold at the celebrated Widecombe Fair. The handsome tower of St Pancras church was built in the late fifteenth century from granite, the local building material. The church is a by-product of a local industry based on mineral veins in local granite: tin. It was local tinners who raised the money for its construction. St Pancras, 'the cathedral of the moor', is a monument to their piety and prosperity.

Loch Brora, Sutherland. In the eighteenth century the people of Sutherland raised goats and black cattle, potatoes and oats. At least five thousand people left this part of the county in the early nineteenth century to make way for sheep.

Overleaf: *Widecombe in the Moor, Devon. Looking down the centuries from the edge of Dartmoor to the tower of St Pancras church.*

1 A Primeval Landscape

The Weald near Goudhurst, Kent. The Weald is a complex geological area with a variety of landforms. The lowland clays have been turned into rich farmland. In the distance is a less fertile ridge of sand planted with forest. The Anglo-Saxon suffix -hurst means wood and indicates how extensive the clearing of woodland for farming has been.

Overleaf: Edinburgh Castle. The castle stands on the neck of an extinct volcano, now choked with solid lava. The surrounding cone of ash has long been worn away.

The surface of the British landscape has been fashioned by man but its form and structure are the product of physical processes operating on a much vaster timescale. The earliest signs of human habitation in Britain are about 20,000 years old; the oldest rocks were formed more than 500 million years ago. If we imagine the evolution of the landscape of Britain compressed into just a week man makes his appearance in the final two minutes. The geological clock ticks very slowly.

Britain has a long and complex geological history. Rocks from all recognized geological periods are present. They have been folded and fractured into a variety of structures and, where exposed at the surface, have been weathered and eroded into a variety of landforms.

Most rocks in Britain were formed under geographical conditions very different from those existing now. The pattern of land and water has changed radically as has the climate. Fossil plants in coal are evidence of the tropical forest swamps that once covered the coalfield regions. Coal measures are interleaved with layers of clay and sandstone, rocks formed by the slow accumulation of river-borne sediment under water. Such sedimentary rocks are laid down horizontally but have since been subject to tilting, buckling and breaking. The contortions of geological structure are often obscured at the surface by erosion and a mantle of soil and vegetation but may be exposed at quarries and cliffs.

Sedimentary rocks are widespread in Britain particularly in southern and eastern England. It is the varying resistances of these rocks to erosion that gives much of England its intimate variety of landform. Softer rocks like clays and sands wash away into gentle slopes and plains while harder limestones and sandstones stand out as steep escarpments. The sudden changes in scenery associated

12

Cader Idris, Snowdonia. The frost-shattered north-east ridge plunges down to a corrie lake. This wild country attracts the hardier, backpacking wanderer.

with these variations are most apparent travelling south-east to north-west across the grain of England's geology. In the Weald, one of the country's most complex geological areas, they occur in all directions.

The oldest and most resistant rocks are generally found in the north and west of Britain, especially in the upland areas of Scotland, Wales, the Lake District and the south-west peninsula. These rocks cooled from molten material, either like granite deep within the earth's crust or like basalt abruptly as lava flowed into

*Llanberis Pass, Snowdonia. Looking towards a U-shaped, glaciated valley –
North Wales is the classic ground for observing glacial features.*

Overleaf: *Wastwater from Scafell Pike in the Lake District. At 3162 feet the
highest mountain in England, Scafell Pike is part of the central peaks of the Lake
District from which the long glacial lakes radiate like the spokes of a wheel. The
most spectacular screes in England plunge into Wastwater on its south-eastern
shore.*

Opposite: *Swallow Falls, Betws-y-Coed. These are caused by the deepening of a valley by glaciation, and are now one of the principal tourist attractions in Snowdonia.*

Above: *Gordale Scar, North Yorkshire. This gorge may have resulted from a collapse of the roof of a former cavern. It became a popular site for tourists and painters when wild country was first being admired in the early nineteenth century.*

Overleaf: *Bridestones, North Yorkshire. Made of millstone grit and sculpted by the wind: there is still no agreement among geomorphologists as to how they were formed. They may have protruded above a former seabed.*

21

fissures and spilled onto the surface. Molten material also baked and altered the rocks through which it passed. Thus former clays and shales in Snowdonia were turned into slates.

Folding which created the hills and valleys of southern England was the gentle, outer rippling of the last period of mountain-building that also produced the Alps. The mountains of Scotland and Wales are much older but have been worn down to mere stumps of their former size. The rugged grandeur of these areas is the result of the geologically recent effects of ice.

After the beginning of history ice covered Britain north of a line from the Bristol Channel to the Thames estuary. The rounded summits of the highest Scottish mountains suggest that the Highlands were completely covered. The frost-shattered summits of Welsh peaks such as Snowdon and Cader Idris indicate that they were, at least for a time, exposed. Valleys were gouged by glaciers. Their sheer sides are now laced with tumbling streams and waterfalls. At higher altitudes where the glaciers originated ice scooped out deep hollows known as 'cirques', now often filled with lakes. Where glaciers ate back into a mountain mass the cirques met in knife-edged ridges and pyramidal peaks. These provide the most breathtaking walks in Britain. When the ice melted and retreated it dumped the material it had plucked and pulverized. Some of this material blocked the mouths of valleys and impounded the long narrow lakes which are such distinctive features of the glaciated highlands of Britain.

Water is the main agent of erosion in Britain. Falling rain washes away finer particles and dissolves less stable minerals. In limestone country it seeps into fissures and through a combination of chemical reaction and physical abrasion hollows out underground watercourses and caverns. The spectacular limestone scenery of Cheddar Gorge and Gordale Scar is thought to result from the roof of a line of caverns collapsing. Water soaking into crevices may also freeze and so expand, widening them. In highland areas successive freezing eventually splits off great blocks from mountain-sides. These fall and shatter forming a mantle of boulders and rocks known as 'scree'.

Apart from some remnants of post-Ice Age forest, no natural vegetation now grows in Britain. The heather and grass moorland which blankets a third of the country looks primeval but is in fact the result of forest clearance to provide wood, charcoal or grazing land. Farmers maintain moorland. Left to itself it will revert to scrub woodland within sixty years. But no one can deny the wild appearance of moorland, which holds visitors spellbound. The moorland of Britain is zealously guarded by the custodians of the nation's landscape heritage; ten National Parks exist to protect it. Aflame with golden gorse and purple heather the moors make spectacular scenery. It is less their purely visual than their evocative qualities which are so alluring. An imagination cramped in a congested city takes flight over these open, windswept uplands.

24

2 Signs of Settlements

Evidence of the earliest settlement of Britain is rarely visible on the land surface. Excavations of post-glacial gravel deposits have revealed stone weapons and tools, the remains of hunting-gathering groups who moved into Britain after the final retreat of the ice sheet about twenty thousand years ago. They moved through a bleak landscape of bog, lakes and tundra. As the climate improved so grasses and then broadleaved woodland took hold. The thickening forests harboured wolves, lynx, bears and numerous deer. These animals, and human settlers, had migrated by land. Britain was not severed from the continental land mass until about 5000 BC. Glacial meltwaters helped raise sea levels and create the English Channel and the southern North Sea. Logs caught in the nets of North Sea trawlers indicate a former plain where the Thames and the Rhine both meandered.

As Britain became an island so men made their first significant marks on its terrain. They avoided thickly forested valleys and claylands but farmed the more open uplands: the Cotswolds, Dartmoor, Salisbury Plain, the Yorkshire Wolds. They grew crops in small fields but made a more lasting impression with their livestock. Controlled grazing and manuring began man's modification of Britain's vegetation.

The five millennia before Roman rule saw the building of striking monuments: megalithic tombs and longbarrows, and later stone circles. Generations of artists, tourists, scholars and cranks have been drawn to Stonehenge. It has the symbolic power of the Pyramids. The images etched into chalk downland – the white horses of Westbury and Uffington, the rampant giant of Cerne Abbas – are the more recent monuments. They were made by the societies the Romans encountered: iron-using farmers living in stable villages administered from and defended by hill forts.

Overleaf: *Stonehenge, Wiltshire. Its building from c. 1900–1500 BC was a vast undertaking. The bluish stones of the outer ring were brought from Pembrokeshire two hundred miles away, probably floated around the coast on rafts and hauled on land on a bed of logs. The design of Stonehenge is now regarded as highly sophisticated but its original purpose remains obscure. It was probably an astronomical observatory, perhaps a temple, maybe both.*

Avebury, Wiltshire. The village has obliterated the pattern of the inner circle of stones. The outer circle is visible now marked with stones replacing the originals which have long since disappeared. Avebury circle was re-discovered in the seventeenth century.

Overleaf: *Uffington, Oxfordshire. The white horse is etched in the chalk, measuring 360 feet from head to tail. No one knows for sure how it got there. To the right is the moat of an early Iron Age fort surrounded by the more shadowy remains of Iron Age fields.*

Britain was on the periphery of the Roman Empire and the Romans were more intent on controlling it than settling it. They constructed a network of well-equipped ports, fortified towns and military posts linked by direct roads. It is a familiar imperial design, one used in India and East Africa by Britain during its ascendancy as a world power.

Apart from some reclamation of salt-marsh on the south-east coast and some cultivation around villas in the 'civil zone' of lowland England, the Romans made little extensive impact on the landscape of Britain. Roads were the arteries of Roman rule but had little economic or social connection with the country they passed through. On either side of them was a native landscape of farms, villages and trackways or, more usually, vast tracts of forest and moor. The roadside was the frontier of Roman civilization. The frontier of Roman rule extended occasionally to the Forth and the Clyde but was finally marked by Hadrian's Wall built across the country from the mouth of the Tyne to the Solway Firth. The Romans conquered Wales but the highland areas of north and west Britain were always a military zone.

The most significant legacies of Roman rule in the landscape are the roads and towns. Some Roman roads like the Fosse Way and Watling Street are the basis of major roads today. Minor roads and bridal paths follow the course of others. The Romans built new towns like York and Chester in strategic military locations. Few of the towns they established have failed to survive.

When the Roman legions finally withdrew in AD 383 they left most of Britain as untouched and untamed as it was after the final retreat of the ice sheet. Because of the scarcity of written records and surviving buildings the aftermath of Roman rule is still sometimes known as the Dark Ages. But if we think of culture in terms of its root meaning – cultivation – then the achievement of the Anglo-Saxons seems much more impressive than that of the Romans. It was they who began to clear the forest, reclaim moorland and marsh and bring heavy soils under the plough. In so doing they established almost every English village existing today. They came to settle, not merely to rule.

'The grey haired enemy of the wood' is an Anglo-Saxon phrase for a ploughman, an image of the time and toil it took to make a clearing and cultivate it. Some families pioneered alone especially on the poorer lands of the north and west. Over much of the country the work was done co-operatively. Each village was surrounded by large open fields in which individuals were granted strips of land and rough pasture where individuals had grazing rights. Decisions on where, when and what to cultivate were made collectively. The working and appearance of this open-field landscape has all but disappeared. Only at Laxton in Nottinghamshire does it survive.

Chysauster, Cornwall. Courtyard houses in a Celtic settlement occupied from the 1st century BC to the 5th–6th century AD.

Overleaf, left: *The remains of a Roman road over Blackstone Edge in the Pennines. It was laboriously paved with flat flagstones. The Romans had not discovered the art of creating a hard surface with rubble.*

Overleaf, right: *Hadrian's Wall at Housesteads. Backed by a string of military camps and fortified settlements and with a look-out tower every mile it was effectively a long thin garrison town. At Housesteads, the ancient Vercovicium, is one of the best preserved of the garrison forts.*

Eskdale from Hardknott Pass in Cumbria. The remains of a Roman fort, Mediobogum ('in the middle of the bend') are on a rise in the foreground.

3 From Medieval Times

The organization and appearance of Britain after the Norman conquest was influenced by three powerful and sometimes contending interests: the Crown, the nobility and the Church. They controlled most of the country and owned most of it too.

Although the Normans came to Britain as overlords with little direct interest in farming they profoundly influenced the development of the countryside. To establish their rule they not only built castles but extended and formalized a manorial system which had existed before the conquest in parts of eastern England. They were not successful in imposing a manorial regime over much of Wales. In parts of England farming villages retained their independence. In both manorial and non-manorial communities rights of ownership, use of and access to land were complex. What is clear is that land was rarely private property as we understand it. Land was 'held' rather than owned outright. The lord of the manor was something less than a landowner, the peasant something more than a tenant.

In some parts of England landlords encouraged the clearing and draining of land for agriculture, in others they discouraged it to create vast hunting 'forests', areas usually but not always wooded. By the reign of Henry II nearly a third of England was set aside as Royal Forest. The destruction of villages and farmland to create the New Forest was an early example of depopulation of the countryside for noble pleasure. Other forest areas continued to be farmed but any new clearing and cultivation had to be officially sanctioned and paid for. Illegal hunting was savagely punished.

Among the largest and most powerful medieval landlords were religious orders. From the early twelfth century the Cistercians changed the face of their estates, clearing woodland and draining marsh on a large scale and creating vast sheep granges especially in the Yorkshire Dales and parts of Wales. In the interests of

38

profitable sheep raising they too were willing to sacrifice villages and farms.

By the middle of the fourteenth century there were over five hundred monasteries, priories, abbeys and cathedrals. The ruins of abbeys such as Fountains, Rievaulx and Tintern, testify to the majesty of the medieval church and the power that broke it. Henry VIII championed their study as historical monuments. The gentry who appropriated the lands on which they stand used them as ornaments for their parks. So fashionable did ruins become in the eighteenth century that new ones were built. The remains of Tintern Abbey satisfied most tourists and artists but not the influential William Gilpin who suggested breaking off bits here and there to make it more 'picturesque'.

The authority of the medieval church was made manifest in most villages. Churches built in Anglo-Saxon times were basically log huts with thatched roofs. Between 1350 and 1500 most were rebuilt in stone with towers and spires. Many new churches were built. These churches expressed not just the ascendancy of the Church but also the growing affluence of those who paid for them: landlords, merchants and wealthy peasants.

The growth of trade stimulated the building of market towns. Old Roman roads were restored, new bridges built, footpaths trodden and trampled into broad tracks. But transport remained laborious and expensive and this made it necessary to create many points of exchange. Some villages were granted market charters, some market towns were newly planned. The lure of rents, tolls and taxes began a fever of speculation in new towns during the twelfth and thirteenth centuries. All major landlords joined in: nobles, Bishops and Kings. Stratford upon Avon was founded in 1196 by the Bishop of Worcester; Portsmouth two years earlier by Richard I.

Oxford and Cambridge were unremarkable market towns before the establishment of their universities in the first years of the thirteenth century. Initially the universities were small groups of scholars meeting in private houses and staying in lodgings. They did not make a tangible impact on the townscapes of Oxford and Cambridge until the building of colleges in the later thirteenth century. The early colleges were essentially ecclesiastical communities, endowed by monks and Bishops and concentrating on the study of theology. They housed, instructed and disciplined their members, and owned their own buildings as well as estates in the country. The familiar collegiate plan of quadrangle, hall, library and chapel developed piecemeal at the first English college, Merton in Oxford. The colleges outstripped the university as corporate bodies and by the sixteenth century were the recognized centres of learning.

In 1348 Britain suffered a devastating invasion: bubonic plague, the Black Death. Population was culled by over a third. The economy lay in ruins. In the largest towns buildings fell empty and grass grew in the streets. Villages shrank and over 1300 were

Bolton Abbey, North Yorkshire. This was established by Augustinian canons. After its dissolution in 1540 it was acquired by the Cavendish family, from 1694 the Dukes of Devonshire. It became a noted beauty spot and was frequently painted by eighteenth- and nineteenth-century watercolourists.

Overleaf: *Abbotsbury, Dorset. Founded by the local Benedictine monastery, after the dissolution it became just a sleepy village.*

eventually deserted. Some villagers died, others left. Where labour was too scarce to maintain arable farming landlords let fields of corn and barley tumble down to rough pasture and evicted any remaining peasants. Vast sheep-runs were created tended only by a few shepherds. By the end of the fifteenth century there were three times as many sheep as men in the kingdom. Sir Thomas More complained bitterly: 'sheep have become so great devourers . . . that they eat up and swallow down the very men themselves. They consume, destroy and devour whole fields, houses and cities'. England became a greener, but, for a time, perhaps less pleasant land.

Thundersley Church, Essex. This was probably the site of a Danish fort. Thundersley means the 'clearing of Thunor', a heathen god. The site was claimed by the Church in the Middle Ages but the present church is an amalgam of later building.

4 Fortified Territory

Medieval Britain was studded with castles. In the twenty years after the conquest of 1066 five hundred were built to rivet Norman rule. The earliest Norman castles were simple structures. They were usually made of wood, often brightly painted and built on a natural prominence or a mound made with earth excavated from a surrounding ditch. As soon as nobles could afford to they rebuilt in stone. In the next two centuries castles became stronger and more elaborate, with sophisticated systems of defence. In the late thirteenth century Edward I established a series of impressive stone fortresses along the coastal plain of North Wales as part of his programme to stamp the authority of the English Crown. Castles like Harlech and Caernarfon with their keeps and battlements are as much a part of our mental picture of the Middle Ages as the great cathedrals and abbeys.

Castles were the military posts of the manorial system. In return for their manors nobles were obliged to raise armed men for the King. When the Crown was weak nobles were ready to raise armies for themselves. Particularly after the Black Death there were outbreaks of private warfare and a wave of new castle building. During the country's recovery nobles established positions to secure or extend their own power against other nobles or the King. With unreliable mercenaries in the ranks of their armies and within the walls of their castles nobles had to secure their personal safety against a mutiny. This is reflected in castle design with the keep, the personal quarters of the family secure against attack from within.

In the later Middle Ages Scotland had an even more martial appearance. Especially in the north-east, rivalries between a large number of small baronies resulted in a high density of castles and fortified houses.

The landscape around surviving castles has now changed so

Corgarff Castle, Grampian, commanded routes through the passes of the rivers Dee, Avon and Don. In the eighteenth century it was used by the Hanoverians to control a disaffected region. Then the star-shaped ramparts were built to permit a wide range of fire.

46

radically that it is often difficult to appreciate their past strategic significance. This is especially true in lowland areas where surrounding forests and bogs have been turned into a tame landscape of farmland and streams. In highland and coastal areas the commanding authority of castles is still immediately evident.

Castle building for military purposes declined because the Tudors re-established the authority of the Crown and judiciary and also because the conventions of war changed. Field battles replaced castle sieges as the main form of military engagement. The capture of a castle became a symptom of victory not its primary aim. This is not to say that castles became irrelevant to military campaigns. During the English Civil War they were occupied and besieged by both Royalists and Parliamentarians. Cromwell's troops dismantled many.

Castles cast a spell on the British imagination long after the era of castle building ended. Houses continued to be built with castellated features when there was no functional need for them. They were an image of security, as in the proverb 'An Englishman's home is his castle', first uttered as a legal precept in the seventeenth century. They also symbolized authority and order, especially valued at times when authority was contested.

> The rich man in his castle,
> The poor man at his gate,
> God made them high or lowly
> And order'd their estate.

These lines were written in 1848, a year of social unrest. The Victorians worshipped both the industrial future and an idealized medieval past. Fanfares of turrets, towers and battlements were added to a variety of new buildings from bridges to railway stations. Country houses were built in a baronial style. The most famous was the royal residence at Balmoral. The most imposing was Penryn Castle in Bangor, built with the profits from local slate mines.

Compared to most continental countries Britain has since the Middle Ages been little scarred by war. A military presence has seldom been conspicuous in the landscape. A long tradition of opposition to State power by both gentry and commoners has resisted it, and this is still true today. Lovers of Dartmoor complain vociferously if army vehicles damage prehistoric evidence and shells hole Sites of Special Scientific Interest. Some signs are inescapable, for example the white spheres on Fylingdales Moor, eerie enough, even impressive: their function is to be part of an early warning system against attack in a war that would reduce the landscape of Britain and other countries to 'a republic of insects and grass'. For the present, however, they contribute to that variety of landscape features, natural and man-made, which makes Britain for the traveller, the most rewarding area of its size to be found anywhere.

Lindisfarne Castle. A fort was first built here in 1542 against the Scots but saw little military action. The present structure was largely built in the early twentieth century as a domestic castle by Sir Edwin Lutyens, the leading country-house architect.

Overleaf: *Harlech Castle. This was built in the late thirteenth century with a sophisticated system of encircling defences. It overlooked the sea but silting has left it dry as well as high. During the Wars of the Roses it was a Lancastrian stronghold, its soldiers celebrated in the marching song 'Men of Harlech'.*

Caerphilly Castle, Glamorgan. Its site on low-lying land has little strategic authority, and the man-made defences were massive and sophisticated. The castle covers thirty acres.

Castle Campbell, Dollar. Sited between the Burns of Care and Sorrow it was appropriately named Castle Gloom until its name was changed by Act of Parliament for the Campbell family. The present buildings date from the fifteenth century.

Overleaf: Dunnottar Castle, Stonehaven. Dunnottar stands on a red sandstone promontory jutting out into the North Sea. The spine joining it to the mainland was cut away to a thin ridge to prevent access.

Bodiam Castle, Kent. It was built in the late fourteenth century as part of a national defence against the threat of French invasion. Dismantled by Parliamentarians, it was admired as a picturesque ruin in the eighteenth century. It was restored in this century.

Overleaf: *Balmoral Castle. Balmoral was built by Prince Albert in the 1850s with locally quarried granite. Still today a private residence of the royal family, it demonstrates the romantic appeal which the castellated style held for the Victorians.*

Menwith Hill Station, North Yorkshire. Part of the NATO early warning system.

5 A Picturesque Country

Half-timbered cottages in a patchwork of fields; a country house in wooded parkland – some of the most picturesque scenes were created between the sixteenth and eighteenth centuries. Such scenes are often felt to represent Olde England, and compared with the look of much of Britain today, perhaps they do. But in fact they also express conventions that, in contrast to those of medieval England, are recognizably modern: private property and enterprise, investment in farming and trade. For the Tudors the Norman conquest was as remote as Shakespeare's England is to us.

From Tudor to Georgian times the English countryside was extensively re-organized and rebuilt. One of the most striking changes was the enclosure of open field and common into compact farms with rectangular fields. The date, pace, scale and method of enclosure varied greatly. In Tudor times it proceeded in a gradual and piecemeal fashion through agreements among freeholders and also suddenly, comprehensively and coercively where the land was owned by a powerful few. In the eighteenth and nineteenth centuries, enclosing landlords were armed with Acts of Parliament. Smallholders gained little from the change; cottagers eking out a living on the edge of the common lost what little they had. Upland pastures were also enclosed, often by walls made of stones cleared from the fields. Only one open-field arable village remains in England but there are still some 400,000 hectares of common grazing land.

Hedged fields have long been contentious features in the landscape. For the poet John Clare, writing during the enclosure of his parish of Helpston in the early nineteenth century, they were part of a process of redevelopment that had abolished familiar landmarks and destroyed his sense of place. Agricultural writers of his time admired them, seeing them as signs of more

Edale in the Peak District.

Enclosed fields near Paignton, Devon. Over much of Devon the country was enclosed by the fourteenth century, either from open field or, by pioneering farmers, from woodland or moor. In the nineteenth century the country around Paignton became nationally renowned for producing a sweet cabbage.

efficient farming methods, besides being more pictorial than the landscape of open fields. Since the war the removal of hedges, estimated at some five thousand miles, has provoked as much argument as their construction. Farmers now argue that hedges are an impediment to efficient farming. Modern machinery and grazing methods demand large unbounded fields. Hedges are now costly to maintain. Opposing farmers are lovers of scenery and ecologists alarmed by the destruction of a habitat for plants and wildlife. Some of the scenic arguments which appeal to the 'traditional' appearance of the English countryside are based, perhaps, on a foreshortened idea of its evolution. In some peripheral counties of England pioneering medieval farmers enclosed fields directly from the waste; but in parts of eastern England the hedges are barely a hundred years old. Land here was farmed on an open-field system for sometimes 1500 years.

Parliamentary enclosure was not necessarily accompanied by more efficient farming but by the early nineteenth century England certainly had a more cultivated appearance. Improved farming meant new crops and rotations, the draining and irrigation of land, the marling of soils, the use of machinery. The Fens and the Weald were reclaimed for agriculture. In the Fens this involved a struggle not just against water but against fiercely independent communities who had for generations made a living from this watery landscape.

The first unfortified country houses were built in the early sixteenth century. Relieved of the need to build for defence their owners now built for pleasure, comfort and display. They did so with fortunes swelled by monastic spoils and profits from the wool trade. One of the earliest, Compton Wynyates in Warwickshire, was built on newly enclosed land on the site of a deserted village, with the bricks of a castle built twenty miles away a century before on the site of another deserted village. The wealth and power of the gentry reached its height in the eighteenth century. Revenues from trade and high office purchased broad acres. Property, the basis of power, was protected by a penal code which seems harsh to our eyes. Grandiose mansions commanded extensive views of vast estates.

The style of country houses changed dramatically between the sixteenth and the eighteenth centuries. Elaborate, sometimes haphazard-looking Tudor palaces gave way to a plainer and more symmetrical style more deeply influenced by classical architecture. Brick was replaced by stone or covered in stucco. Country houses of the older style were often reconstructed or merely clothed in the new.

Changes in the surroundings of country houses were more radical. The eighteenth-century taste for landscaping often erased exquisite Tudor gardens with their elaborate knots and parterres and also the large-scale geometrical designs of the seventeenth century inspired by the example of palatial French gardens, especially Versailles. Landscape parks are much admired and may

even be mistaken, as they were half intended to be, as works of nature not works of art. The most famous designer was Lancelot 'Capability' Brown, so called because he recognized the capability of a park becoming a tasteful-looking landscape. The making of landscape parks was often a vast and expensive undertaking. Hills were levelled, others built; trees uprooted, others planted; streams diverted, lakes created. Now matured, their beauty may obscure not just their artifice but also the broader effects of their construction. Brown's clients did not hesitate to remove footpaths, roads, watermills, churches, farms and occasionally whole villages to improve the view. They were, in their own time, criticized for this. Brown's successor, Humphry Repton, practised a smaller-scale, less disruptive style of landscape gardening. He was no less intent on creating agreeable scenery but was more tolerant of established features, whether old gardens or villages.

Some of the most attractive smaller houses in England were built during these prosperous years from the sixteenth to eighteenth centuries. Tradesmen and yeomen farmers demanded more comfortable houses. They demolished or rebuilt medieval houses. Living space was enlarged, often with the addition of upper storeys, and divided into specialized rooms with fireplaces and glazed windows. This provided the modern domestic amenities of privacy, warmth and light. In the eighteenth century the building of individual houses in regional vernacular styles gave way to the building or refacing of whole streets and squares in academically approved styles and materials.

The appearance of English villages is influenced by many factors: the ownership of land, the pattern of landholding, the type of agriculture and, more recently, the policies of conservationists. A uniformity of style and materials may indicate that a village is owned by one landowner and built over a short period. A longer history and more fragmented pattern of ownership is often the basis for a more varied and picturesque scene: a medieval church, a Victorian rectory, a row of Tudor almshouses, a Georgian manse.

Enclosed pastures near Malham, Yorkshire. The drystone walls are of local limestone.

The gardens of Edzell Castle, Tayside. The Department of the Environment has here restored a garden built in 1604. With the sculptures in the walls and the formal bedding the garden forms a Renaissance 'pleasance', a place to stroll and contemplate the moral and mythical symbolism of the design.

Opposite: *Wicken Fen, Cambridgeshire. Once thought to be a surviving example of natural fen vegetation it is now known to have been extensively modified by peat digging and sedge cutting. It is now a nature reserve.*

Audley End, Essex. The early seventeenth-century house and formal park were remodelled in the eighteenth century. The park was landscaped by 'Capability' Brown. The work cost £100,000, well over a million pounds in today's currency. Fifty gardeners were needed to maintain the grounds.

Stowe, Buckinghamshire. Now a
public school, Stowe and its park
are among the greatest monuments
to eighteenth-century architecture
and the 'Natural Style' in
gardening. Important to such
'created' landscapes were artfully
placed architectural features,
temples and the like, often
designed by the greatest
practitioners of the day.
Vanbrugh, Kent, Gibbs and
Adam all worked at Stowe.
Capability Brown started here.

6 Buildings in a Landscape

In the waves of building and rebuilding from the sixteenth
to eighteenth centuries many could afford to build well but all
but the most affluent used local materials and skills because of
the expense of transporting them from afar. This resulted in
some of the most agreeable scenes in Britain. Buildings of local
material are the man-made expression of the local physical
geography and often congenial to the landscape: buildings of
limestone in the Cotswolds, flint in Norfolk, granite and thatch in
Dartmoor, timber and brick in the Midlands.

Until the seventeenth century wood was the most popular
building material. It was readily available and easily handled. But
wood is more perishable than stone or brick and few timber
buildings from before the seventeenth century have survived.
Since then the most common method of using wood was 'half-
timbering': skeletons of hardwood beams and rafters in a casing of
sticks were filled in with mud or plaster. Shrewsbury and Chester
are among English towns with a profusion of half-timbered
buildings but it is sometimes difficult to tell the genuine article
from bogus reconstructions. Every pre-war suburb has its 'Tudor
style' family homes and villages throughout the country contain
modern pubs, tea rooms and antique shops covered in black
planks and white plaster.

The depletion of woodlands and the risk of fire encouraged the
use of stone for building new houses and rebuilding or recasing
old ones. In the Cotswolds buildings of creamy limestone are the
prominent features of the landscape: churches, houses, cottages,
farm-buildings, walls. Between the fifteenth and eighteenth
centuries there was abundant freestone – almost every village had
its quarry – and abundant money from the wool trade to pay for
it. If the Cotswolds are the rural showplace for limestone
building, Bath is surely the urban one. Few other freestones have

*Eynsford, Kent. Though now
by-passed by a small bridge, the
'ford' at Eynsford leads towards
the villa at Lullingstone, one of
the most remarkable Roman sites,
where once stood a country house.
Lullingstone has made a great
contribution to our knowledge of
the Romans' private life.*

77

the charm of limestone. Granite is not as good a reflector of light, scarcely weathers and is not easy to work artistically. It imparts an atmosphere of strength and severity to cities where it is used extensively. Granite buildings can look picturesque. In the combes of Devon moorstone cottages are softened by thatch and luxuriant gardens. Perhaps the most unredeemable stone is slate. In the slate-mining areas of North Wales it is used as ubiquitously as limestone is in the Cotswolds, and on a wet day deepens an already sombre scene.

The first bricks were fired by the Romans but a brick-making industry was not established in Britain until the fourteenth century. Bricks have many advantages: they are cheap to make, easy to build with and very durable. They can also be colourful. Shades from yellow to grey reflect the varying impurities of local clays. The use of brick did not become widespread until the tax on them was repealed in the nineteenth century and brick-making was mechanized. Mass-produced red bricks are not as attractive as some hand-made varieties but they helped house the inhabitants of the new industrial cities.

Revolutions in transportation cheapened the carriage of building materials. The canals and finally the railways spelled the end of local building materials and building traditions. This was not necessarily a bad thing. In 1782 an observer noted the influence of the Trent and Mersey Canal on building: 'the cottage instead of being half covered in miserable thatch is now covered with a substantial covering of tiles and slates brought from the distant hills of Wales or Cumberland'. Slate roofs became more widespread when the tax on slate was repealed in 1831. Slate from the great quarries of North Wales was in heavy demand. It cleaved smoothly and was easily trimmed into standard rectangles.

The taste for vernacular building styles and materials has not diminished – if anything, the contrary is the case. In the commuter villages of the Home Counties and around other large cities money earned in offices of concrete and glass is lavished on cottages of cob and thatch, and the skills required in the maintenance and restoration of vernacular buildings are more in demand than they have been for decades.

The Cross, Chester. Chester has one of the country's highest concentrations of genuine 'black and white' half-timbered buildings. The Rows, raised walkways with shops at street and upper-floor level, have existed in some form for at least six centuries.

Overleaf: *Half-timbering with literary associations: Shakespeare's birthplace at Stratford-upon-Avon.*

A weird and abstract landscape: stone quarries between Newlyn and Mousehole, Cornwall.

Opposite: *Buckland in the Moor, Dartmoor, Devon: cottages of granite with complementary grey thatch huddle in a picture-postcard setting.*

Overleaf: *The spoil tip of a slate mine at Blaenau Ffestiniog, North Wales, dwarfs the cottages of those who dumped it. There have been large-scale workings here since the mid-eighteenth century. Production reached a peak around 1900. Since the war it has declined steeply.*

7 Industrial Grandeur

The Industrial Revolution had a profound effect on the landscape of Britain and one more varied than the conventional image of satanic mills darkening green pastures. Before the Industrial Revolution Britain was not entirely agricultural. Cloth-making was well established, iron-founding and glass-making too. Industry occupied parts of towns and whole villages, and flourished among fields and forests seeking seasonal reserves of labour and raw materials.

Until the later eighteenth century industry was usually scattered and small in scale. The first area of industrial concentration was established around Coalbrookdale in Shropshire near the Severn Gorge. Here innovations in the making and use of iron made a striking impact on the landscape. Tourists, artists and industrial spies came to observe the flaring foundries and the world's first single-span bridge made entirely of iron.

Changes in the scale and methods of industrial production were pronounced, sometimes dramatic, but the timing, pace, and location of these changes varied greatly even within one industry. By the early nineteenth century steam-powered mills filled West Yorkshire valleys spinning yarn that was still woven on handlooms in upland hamlets. When weaving was mechanized and railways built, small mill colonies expanded into factory towns.

Industrial towns did not expand indiscriminately. Pre-industrial patterns of land use and ownership shaped their development. Rows of 'back to backs' followed the course of medieval footpaths and field boundaries. Aristocratic landowners both promoted and obstructed the urban development of their estates. At Nottingham the maintenance of an open-field system around the town until

1845 throttled its expansion and by intensifying overcrowding within the city helped create some of the worst slums in Britain.

The living and working conditions of industrial towns justifiably alarmed contemporaries. Here and there a humane employer provided some decent houses, sometimes a small park. Only government legislation guaranteed minimum environmental standards for life and work. Programmes of public building added some grandeur to an often bleak landscape. Much of the Victorian fabric of towns and cities has been demolished but some palatial town halls, banks and railway stations remain. Little urban building since expresses such civic confidence and pride.

Victorian textile mills are now seen to be as much a part of Britain's heritage as stately homes. Their widespread destruction in the past twenty years has provoked calls for their preservation. Local authorities now seek alternative uses for them when textile firms close. Some now house industrial museums. There is now a taste for old industrial landscape. L. S. Lowry is now as popular a landscape painter as Constable. Constable made the Agricultural Revolution pictorial, Lowry the Industrial Revolution.

Canals and railways articulated the Industrial Revolution. They made a notable, sometimes dramatic, impact on the landscape. The Duke of Bridgewater pioneered aristocratic involvement in industry when, in 1780, he employed James Brindley to design a canal from the coal mines at Worsley to Manchester. It bridged roads and valleys and tunnelled through hills. Later canals took even more direct routes and included more daring feats of engineering: subterranean junctions, soaring aqueducts and flights of locks.

The railways made a greater and more extensive impact. They transformed the relation between travel and terrain. They were built through the landscape not upon it. The deep cuttings and high embankments have been hailed as the greatest earthworks since the Iron Age of pre-Roman times. They astonished contemporaries. It is now difficult to imagine the disruption railway building caused. The terror that the navvies inspired in the country has long been forgotten and the embankments are now mantled in green. The disruption near city terminals was more severe – whole districts were cleared.

Passenger traffic on the railways expanded rapidly. Victorians discovered the first form of travel that could frequently be a pleasure in itself. The ride was steady and comfortable with leisure to admire the new views the railway exposed. The railway hastened industrial development but also helped transform farming landscapes. The speedy carriage of milk and livestock encouraged the creation of new pasture and the cheap transport of manure improved arable land. The railway opened up previously remote areas for leisure. The line to the shores of Windermere allowed northern industrialists to live in the Lake District at weekends and their workers to visit on daytrips. The elderly Wordsworth complained bitterly.

As the building of railways hastened the decline of canals so the building of motorways and improvement of trunk roads hastened the railways' decline. In the 1960s many local lines were amputated from the network. Now eighty per cent of all passenger traffic is by private car and a similarly high proportion of freight is carried by road. The car manufacturers, road-haulage companies and oil companies now exert the power that the old rail companies did. The motorway system is now some 1500 miles long. Bulging at intersections and service stations it forms an extensive landscape of its own. Pressure groups now resist new construction. When the M5 was extended to the West Country fears were expressed that the masses of Birmingham and the Black Country would descend on Dartmoor. A stretch in Kent was resisted because it was routed through an area made famous by the landscape painter Samuel Palmer. Time and taste have rendered railways picturesque as well as enclosed fields and factories. Motorways too may well be absorbed into the landscape and our liking for it.

The most ethereal structures of the motorway age are the suspension bridges built across the estuaries of the Severn, Forth and Humber. The latest, the Humber Bridge, is the largest in the world and, like the Iron Bridge in the eighteenth century, is promoted as a tourist attraction. Viewing points are provided, the surroundings are landscaped, and ice creams and hamburgers are on sale.

The Iron Bridge, a symbol of the early Industrial Revolution. Technology had not yet fully adapted to the properties of the new material. The shape and proportions of the Iron Bridge over the Severn recall masonry bridges. Carpentry techniques such as wedges and dovetail joints were used to connect the parts. It was not an entirely functional structure. Its appearance was enhanced by decorative iron work. The owners of the Iron Bridge appreciated its striking visual qualities. They promoted it as a motif for publicizing the area. It appeared on numerous prints, bill headings, coins and pottery. Now it is the centrepiece of an open-air industrial museum.

Railway and canal viaducts near Preesgweene. The Chirk canal viaduct shown here was designed by Thomas Telford to carry the Shropshire Union Canal.

Opposite: Aberdare, Mid Glamorgan. In the mid-nineteenth century it was crowded with iron works and collieries and some of the worst housing in Britain. In the first flush of post-war development new industries were established but the town now shares in the problems suffered by other towns on the South Wales coalfield.

Hebden Bridge, West Yorkshire. A woollen mill town surrounded by moorland hamlets, once inhabited by handloom weavers. Hebden Bridge now exploits the tourist potential of its industrial heritage. Old mills have been rehabilitated and reoccupied by craftsmen and restaurants.

Opposite: *The Shropshire Union Canal at Chester. Many canals are now plied by pleasure craft and some have been repaired and re-opened for this use.*

An intersection of the M85 near Perth. Later motorways were designed to harmonise with the landscapes they passed through and also to provide views for motorists.

Opposite: *Railway viaduct near Betwys-y-Coed. Note the battlements! Vegetation has made it now more picturesque, even, than its builders might have envisaged. Locally quarried slate was used in the construction.*

The Severn Bridge. Completed in 1966, it carries the M4 between south-west England and South Wales reducing the journey by fifty miles. It has a central span of 3240 feet. The cables are made of over 18,000 miles of high-tensile steel wire.

8 The Sea

Britain's coastline is long and its scenery varied. England and Wales alone have 2750 miles of coast and Scotland, with its sea-lochs and fringe of islands, many more. Coastal landforms vary from stormy headlands to placid sands and are put to a variety of uses from coal-mining to holiday-making.

Britain's regional geology is exposed in its coastal scenery. The western coasts are edged by solid rock, those of the east by less coherent sands, gravels and glacial material. Cliffs vary greatly in colour: red sandstones, white chalks, grey granites. Complex bedding and folding of clays, chalks and sands on the south coast have resulted in multi-coloured cliffs.

Geological change is evident at the coast. The sea scours cliffs and pounds rocks to sand. The piling of sand at groynes and breakwaters indicates the instability of beaches. During storm surges they may be entirely swept away. In quiet estuaries rivers dump their loads of silt; mud-flats are colonized by plants; dry land emerges. Deposition and erosion have changed the human geography of coasts. Silting has stranded former ports inland while others lie beneath the waves. On softer rocks erosion is rapid. Some parts of the Norfolk coast recede by as much as fifteen feet a year.

From Tudor times Britain's coasts have played a critical role in its economy. Before the establishment of canals and railways coastal waters were the main means of transporting heavy goods. Overseas trade expanded rapidly beginning with the export of wool, culminating in a complex colonial trade. The Royal Navy extended and defended Britain's commercial empire. Major estuaries were built with docks, warehouses and shipyards. The expansion of sea trade affected scenery inland. Forests were felled for ship-building timber in the seventeenth century and woods planted to renew resources in the eighteenth. Fortunes made from

A seastack off the Caithness coast. The sea has worn down a fault line and prised the stack from the cliff. This is the domain of seal and seabird.

99

seaborne trade were spent purchasing and improving country estates.

London has always been Britain's premier port. Recent excavations have revealed evidence of settlement for some five thousand years. Like many ancient settlements London was established at a fording point. This was the first upstream of a major waterway to the Continent. The Romans recognized the strategic importance of the site. They dredged and embanked a channel for deep-draughted ships, drained marshy land and rebuilt the settlement in stone. They made London a port for the export of British resources: precious metals, hides, slaves. Between Roman and Norman rule the commercial importance of London was maintained. It increased rapidly during the revival of trade in the Middle Ages and reached its height during Britain's colonial supremacy. By the later eighteenth century the river was jammed with ships and lighters unloading them. Existing wharves and warehouses could not cope. Massive new docks were built downstream at Wapping, Blackwall and the Isle of Dogs. Further changes in the volume and nature of cargo have caused many to be abandoned. Tilbury, twenty-six miles downstream from London Bridge, is now the capital's main port.

Commercial fishing villages date from the fifteenth century as do squabbles with other European nations over the use of fishing grounds. Cured herring became part of the British diet and there was a valuable export of salted cod to the Continent. The fishing industry was revolutionized in the nineteenth century by the use of trawling gear and the linking of ports by rail with major towns and cities inland. The railway created Grimsby. Whaling in the polar seas stimulated the growth of Hull and Whitby.

The 'seaside' is a nineteenth-century invention. The Victorians discovered a child's paradise in the world of sand, seaweed, rocks and pools and embellished it with donkey rides and puppet shows. The railway and the establishment of paid holidays opened up coastal resorts to the masses. This resulted in twin resorts, one plebeian, one polite: Brighton and Hove, Margate and Broadstairs, Blackpool and Lytham St Annes.

Pressure on Britain's coasts is greatest nearest the main centres of population. Much of the coast of Scotland shows few signs of human handiwork but that of England and Wales is extensively built over and increasingly fought over. From Portsmouth to the Thames estuary there is scarcely ten miles untouched. Some local authorities now protect coasts of scenic or scientific interest. The National Trust now owns some 420 miles of coastline in England and Wales. The making of the British landscape includes negotiations between men as well as with nature, and these are no less evident at the edge of Britain than in the interior.

Mudflats in the Thames estuary at Canvey Point.

Opposite: *Cliffs at Alum Bay, Isle of Wight. The multi-coloured deposits of clays and sands have been tilted vertically, providing an attraction for tourists and collectors.*

London from the air. The capital has always been Britain's leading port but changes in the volume and nature of freight have necessitated the progressive moving of docks downstream. Most of those in the foreground of the photograph are abandoned or undergoing redevelopment for industry or leisure activities.

Opposite: *Near Lulworth Cove, Dorset. The exposure to marine erosion of rocks of different hardnesses – chalks, clays and limestones – has resulted in this distinctive coastal landform.*

London from the air. The capital has always been Britain's leading port but changes in the volume and nature of freight have necessitated the progressive moving of docks downstream. Most of those in the foreground of the photograph are abandoned or undergoing redevelopment for industry or leisure activities.

Opposite: *Near Lulworth Cove, Dorset. The exposure to marine erosion of rocks of different hardnesses – chalks, clays and limestones – has resulted in this distinctive coastal landform.*

*Whitby. Once a major whaling port, Whitby is now a seaside resort with a small
fishing fleet. The circumnavigator James Cook was apprenticed to a Whitby
shipowner.*

Opposite: *Tilbury. Twenty-six miles downstream from London Bridge,
Tilbury is now the Port of London's major dock site. It handles an increasing
volume of containerized freight.*

Photographers Note

Time was when only a large-format plate camera would have sufficed for high-quality work, but today's medium-format cameras give us the quality necessary for reproduction, and their portability, together with a variety of lenses and the advantage of roll-films' dozen or so images combine to make them my favourite tool. The ground screen is still large enough for one to anticipate final results. The depth-of-field preview button gives a precise indication of depth of field offered by a given lens at a given setting and the precise effect of lens attachments.

In air-to-ground photography the 90° viewing angle of medium-format cameras seems a definite advantage, enabling you to point and shoot out of a high window without too much discomfort.

My favourite camera – and the one most of my photography is produced with – is the now defunct and much underrated Kowa Super 66, together with 40mm wide-angle lens, 85mm standard lens, 150- and 250mm tele lenses, with interchangeable backs and two bodies. A personal fad? Maybe. But it is usually the equipment you're most familiar with that gives you the best results.

From the air, focusing will hardly be a problem – your subject remaining at infinity – nor does depth of field pose particular problems. It is better to open the lens and increase shutter speed to counter camera shake from engine shudder and wind slipstream.

The lack of TTL metering, on the other hand, is a definite disadvantage in aerial photography, as every angle from a circling plane can give a different reading, particularly over sunlit water.

Concrete pillbox in Essex. These miniature, defensive fortifications are a frequent reminder in southern England of the last invasion scare. Napoleon never put Martello towers to the test; so, equally, these emplacements never had to prove their worth in the Second World War.

109

Speedy handling of the light meter and camera adjustment are essential.

Choice of film stock is another aspect of personal preference. The fine-grain properties of a slow film are of obvious advantage. For landscape work I find the cool blues and greens of Agfa 50S transparency film preferable, even though I uprate that film to 100 ASA as a rule. That combination has given me my most consistent results to date, after many experiments and disappointments. Reliability of service and consistency of results are naturally governing factors.

Although a tripod tends to accompany me on all my journeys, its actual use is rare, as most photographic vantage points are out of reach of the car and considerable mileage simply has to be covered on foot.

One advantage of the wide-angle lens is its extensive depth of field, permitting a faster shutter speed, and keeping foreground and background in sharp focus – especially important if it is necessary to pick out some historical or botanical foreground feature. Also there is the possibility of including large areas of sky, should cloud formations or coloration be of particular interest. In confined spaces it may be necessary to use its properties carefully, pointing it slightly downwards to place verticals at the top of the frame and so reduce distortion by converging lines. For a realistic impression it is better to 'waste' the lower part of the frame. Alternatively the full effect of converging lines may of course be used dramatically, as in some architectural photography.

The standard lens is precisely what the term implies – the most common or most used lens: in my case the 85mm. To maximize depth of field I make it a rule to set infinity on the distance ring against the chosen f-stop on the display ring, once shutter speed and f-stop have been determined and set. You can then read off from what distance onwards to infinity your picture will be in focus. For instance at f22 focus will commence with the 40mm lens at about 1.6 metres; with the 85mm at about 8 metres and with the 150mm tele at about 22 metres.

The longer the lens you use, the more important is the use of the tripod to counteract camera shake. And do not forget to give that extra stop or two to allow for light loss in the longer 'teles'. Experiment will be your best guide for a particular lens, but if in doubt, 'bracket' exposures. Half a stop or a stop either side of what you consider to be correct may lead to just that little improvement when you compare results afterwards – and all you have lost are a few frames of film. As a general rule, when metering the light value of open landscape, choose the middle setting between the highest reading of the sky and the lowest of the ground. Snow scenes tend to influence the light meter noticeably producing an under-exposed result. Take a reading from a neutral grey subject – if nothing is handy, your hand will do – to compensate for the influence of glare.

If a scene can be improved with a filter without being

110

intrinsically falsified, that seems to me a photographer's option. The haze-filter may bring just that little more clarity, but more than that, as it does no harm, it stays on most of the time as a protection for the lens.

A polarizing filter reduces glare off reflective surfaces and can add depth and drama to the sky if used at right angles to the sun and it can change the colour of the sea to blue or green. Remember it also cuts light values by up to 2 stops.

Half-grey or half-coloured filters accentuate or reinforce an indifferent sky, but are particularly effective when used *contre-jour* to include the sun. A sepia filter may give a traditional scene a more acceptable overall unity of tone. Artists have always changed a scene to suit their own personal style or their story-telling intent, though for the purposes of this book visual alterations have been kept to a minimum.

Composing The Image
You are capturing a three-dimensional scene on a two-dimensional film plane. Looking from the air onto tidal mud with its pattern of drainage rivulets, or onto the age-old pattern of man-made fields, stone-walled enclosures or the now rarer hedges, the two-dimensional element is self-evident and the most important consideration becomes harmony – harmony of colour and design. As a rule nature's colours harmonize well – blues and greens, the rust-brown and mellow shades of autumn. But even when they contrast, they tend to be pleasing because they are natural and we are used to them.

Light falling at an oblique angle across a flat landscape improves pattern and texture by lengthening shadows and so increasing contrast, while emphasizing anything raised or indented. So the pattern of a prehistoric site – a collection of low ridges and bumps seen from ground level – can become an architect's layout from above.

Light is the most important and most powerful ingredient in a successful landscape photograph. Use the cool mists of morning to hold together a many-faceted scene or let the late glow of the evening sun suffuse everything with a golden cast. Let the wide-angle lens with a low horizon collect the full visual force of a cloud build-up before a threatening thunderstorm and catch a sparse sun-beam just as it illuminates some important feature in the middle-distance. The trick is to be in the right spot at the right time . . . anticipation!

Patience, too, can be most rewarding. Anticipate the movement of clouds and with patience they can be used to your advantage. In their varied forms and formations they can be just right for a particular landscape, adding drama or serenity or underlining vastness. The pattern of their shadows on the landscape is of prime pictorial importance.

All landscape photography is a matter of selection – selecting the viewpoint, the time of day or year, selecting the ingredients carefully and the light which falls on them – and leaving out anything that is not compatible with your idea for a particular scene. Most unwanted intrusions are, I find, man-made.

Selection can be aided by your choice of lens or the foreground. If an unwanted foreground feature cannot be avoided, deliberate lack of focus may be the answer. The lighter, brighter object is more likely to draw the viewers' attention than a dark one. A bright colour near the edge of the frame will draw attention away from the centre of interest. Strong converging lines – a road for instance – lead the eye through a picture. Ideally they should lead to a point of interest.

Dissect a picture into three parts, horizontally and also vertically. The four points where those imaginary lines cross near the corners are known as the 'thirds'. It is a principle much beloved by camera clubs that points of interest in a picture are most effective when placed at any of those points . . . the 'rule of the third'.

Framing a picture, by shooting through a doorway or from under the boughs of trees for instance, is a good ploy to prevent the eyes wandering off the edge of the photograph and concentrating attention on the main subject.

Should you include people in your landscape? They may be useful to add scale to a difficult environment. But ideally they should be compatible with the scenery – the farmer in his field, the wanderer on the road or the fell, dressed for mountaineering in high regions. Cars can rarely be avoided in urban scenes, but beware : they can date a picture rather quickly.

It has often been said that the best lighting for landscapes is when the sun shines at an angle over your shoulder, illuminating a scene, yet affording shadows. But try shooting into the sun a. aim for a silhouette – particularly effective at sunset. Bare trees are ideal for such treatment. Trees – and I particularly like their bare winter patterns – are often unavoidable props in the British landscape. From the stunted, wind-shaped forms that seem to echo the shape of the land in coastal regions, to the stately giants in parks or gardens, trees can become symbols of nature's struggle to survive, of abundance, of strength and of impermanence. Bare trees may let you see the buildings that leaves otherwise hide from view.

Nor do you need to stop shooting when the summer colours have gone. Spring, autumn and winter can have beautiful, if different, lighting conditions. It is a mistake to put your camera away for the winter. Those cold, frosty mornings with that lingering mist and the possibility of hoar frost, or the still, windless afternoons, when smoke rises vertically from the country chimneys, are in their way as typical as a daffodil-covered park or a corn-ripe field. Catching those fleeting moments make landscape photography both difficult and popular.

Eskdale, from Hardknott Pass (see pages 36–7), was photographed on the last day of November . . .